HEALTH&
Well-Being

Healthy
Lifestyles

BY GEMMA MᶜMULLEN

BookLife
King's Lynn
Norfolk PE30 4LS

ISBN: 978-1-78637-095-2

All rights reserved.
Printed in Malaysia.

©This edition was published in
2018. First published in 2017.

A catalogue record for this book
is available from the British Library.

Written by:
Gemma McMullen

Edited by:
Grace Jones

Designed by:
Natalie Carr

LOOK FOR THE WORDS LIKE **THIS** IN THE GLOSSARY ON PAGE 31.

Contents

HOW MUCH SLEEP DO YOU NEED?

FIND OUT INSIDE ON PAGE 8.

WHAT CAN HELP YOU TO DEAL WITH STRESS? FEATURED ON PAGE 10.

HEALTHY

HEALTHY BODY

The way that we treat our bodies is extremely important because without good health we would **CEASE** to exist. The food that we eat and the amount that we exercise both contribute massively to the health of our bodies. We need to respect our bodies so that they stay healthy for longer.

WHAT IS HEALTHY LIVING?

ALTHOUGH WE ARE ALL **UNIQUE** OUR BODIES ALL WORK **IN THE** SAME WAY AND NEED THE SAME THINGS TO **STAY** HEALTHY.

HEALTHY living is the term given to the ideal way of living our lives. Put simply, it means that we live our lives in the healthiest way possible. Healthy living relates to every single aspect of our lives, from the things that we eat to the amount that we sleep.

Living

HEALTHY CHOICES

Whilst it is unlikely that a person will always choose the healthiest option, it is important that we take all options into consideration so that we are able to make **INFORMED CHOICES** about the way that we live our lives. This book is about the human body and the ways to keep it healthy.

HEALTHY MIND

The health of our minds is of equal importance to that of our bodies. Our minds control the way that we think and the ways in which we use our bodies. Keeping a healthy mind includes having healthy relationships with others and being able to deal with our problems rationally.

HEALTH AND

WHAT IS WELL-BEING?

The way that we treat our bodies now can have a huge impact on how well they perform in the future and how long they last into adulthood. Eating good food and exercising regularly can go a long way to making sure that our bodies stay healthy. Sleep also plays an important role in our **PHYSICAL** well-being.

THERE are many different aspects of healthy living. Everyone agrees that, in order to have a healthy lifestyle, it is important to think about specific things, such as what you are eating and how much you are exercising. However, there are also more general areas that should be considered when trying to keep ourselves healthy.

Well-Being

MENTAL WELL-BEING

It is just as important to look after our minds as it is to look after our bodies. This can be a far harder task, however, because it can often be difficult to know about our own mental well-being. Making sure that we have healthy relationships goes a long way towards keeping us happy. It is perfectly normal to have worries and problems sometimes, but if these worries and problems start to take over our thoughts, it might be a sign that we should take care of our mental well-being.

IT CAN OFTEN BE A GOOD IDEA TO SHARE YOUR PROBLEMS AND WORRIES WITH A FRIEND THAT YOU CAN TRUST.

KNOW YOUR BODY, KNOW YOUR MIND

If you know your body and your mind well, it can be easier for you to know when one of them is unwell or isn't working properly. If you think that your mind or body is unwell, it's best to ask a parent or guardian for their advice. Many aches, pains and changes to your body are normal as you grow up, but it is still a good idea to check with an adult if you are worried about anything. This also includes any thoughts or feelings that you might have.

Sleep

HOW MUCH SLEEP?

THE amount of sleep that a person needs to get each night depends on how old they are. Young babies need to sleep for around sixteen hours every day, while an adult may only need to sleep for around six hours. Most children need to sleep for around ten hours each night.

WHY DO WE NEED TO SLEEP?

When we sleep, our bodies have a chance to rest. If they need to, the muscles in our legs and arms can repair themselves before they are used again the next day. It is also thought that the **HORMONES** that help us to grow are released at night. However, not every part of the body rests. The brain and heart stay active throughout the night. Scientists believe that the brain uses sleep to process events from the day before so that they can be remembered more clearly.

WHAT HAPPENS IF I DON'T SLEEP?

Believe it or not, the human body can actually last longer without food than it can without sleep. If we don't get enough sleep, we can feel unwell and act angrily towards the people around us. We also might find it harder to focus on our school work and we may find that we become clumsy.

WHAT IF I CAN'T SLEEP?

Most of us will struggle to get a good night's sleep at some point or another. If this happens to you, these tips may help:

TRY HAVING A WARM BATH **BEFORE BED** AND A WARM (**CAFFEINE FREE**) DRINK.

MAKE SURE THAT YOU DO EXERCISE THROUGHOUT THE DAY, SO THAT YOUR BODY IS TIRED WHEN YOU GO TO BED.

HAVE A REGULAR ROUTINE. GOING TO BED AT THE **SAME TIME EACH NIGHT** HELPS THE BODY TO RELAX.

WORRY AND

WHAT IS WORRY AND STRESS?

WHEN we are worried about something, it can sometimes become the only thing that we think about. Thinking about it may cause us to have funny feelings in our stomachs and might make us feel sick. We may even get a headache or feel upset. All of these feelings mean that we are stressed. Both adults and children can feel stressed.

WHAT MIGHT MAKE US FEEL STRESSED?

Lots of things can make us feel stressed and different people will often get stressed by different things. It may be that you have a test or an exam coming up at school and the thought of it makes you nervous. Or it might be that you have had an argument with a friend or a family member at home. These things, as well as lots of other things, can cause people to feel stressed and it can be helpful to talk to someone that you trust if this happens to you.

Stress

WHAT HAPPENS WHEN I AM STRESSED?

LONG-TERM STRESS

Feeling some stress is a normal part of life. In some situations, it can actually be helpful because it can keep us alert and focused. However, when a person feels stressed for a long period of time, it can start to impact on their everyday life. The person may even start to feel unwell because being very stressed can make it easier for you to get ill.

If somebody is feeling stressed, they are often unable to concentrate on anything other than the problem that is worrying them. When someone gets very stressed, other things that are important to them are sometimes affected, such as their school work or their performance on a sports team. People who are stressed also sometimes struggle to sleep. These people might become angry because they are tired and **ANXIOUS**.

DEALING WITH STRESS

THE first step to dealing with stress is to work out what is causing it. There might be only one big problem causing the stress or it may be caused by many smaller worries. Once you know what is causing the stress, you can try to work out the best way to deal with it.

WHAT CAN HELP?

People sometimes feel stressed because they are not very **ORGANISED**. If you are feeling stressed about schoolwork or homework, putting together a timetable of when to do each piece of work can help you to feel better. In the same way, if there is an exam that you are worried about, doing revision will make you feel calmer than just allowing yourself to worry about it.

TALKING ABOUT IT

It often helps to talk about our problems. Talking to a friend or family member that you trust can often help you to work out the best way to deal with your problems. Instead, if the problem is to do with a particular person, talking to them about it can sometimes help. Arguments are sometimes easily solved this way.

IF YOU START TO STRUGGLE WITH THE FEELING OF STRESS, TAKING A FEW LONG, DEEP BREATHS CAN SOMETIMES HELP.

ANYTHING ELSE?

Being healthy in all aspects of your life will help your body and mind to deal with stress in a more **EFFECTIVE** way. Try to make sure that you are eating well, exercising and getting enough sleep. Allow yourself time to relax at home by enjoying a warm bath or reading a book.

KEEPING

WHY SHOULD I KEEP CLEAN?

GERMS are the tiny **ORGANISMS** that cause illness and disease and they are all around us. By keeping ourselves clean, we are less likely to let germs into our bodies and become unwell. We are also less likely to spread germs to other people.

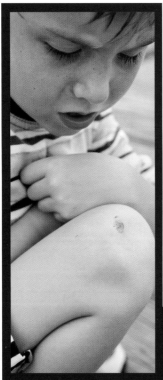

IT IS IMPORTANT TO KEEP CUTS AND GRAZES CLEAN AS OTHERWISE THEY CAN LET GERMS ENTER YOUR BODY.

YOUR SKIN

The skin is the organ that covers the body and it helps to keep out germs. It is important that we keep our skin healthy so that it can do its job. Keeping your skin clean by having a bath or a shower every day helps your skin to stay healthy. Some areas of your skin, such as the skin on your hands, need to be washed more often than others as they will come into contact with more unclean surfaces.

Clean

WHAT IS SWEAT?

When we get hot, **GLANDS** in our skin release a small amount of liquid called sweat, which then dries on our skin. This is a natural reaction that helps our bodies to cool down. Sweat itself does not smell – the smell that we link with sweat comes from the sweat mixing with germs on our skin. Washing our bodies helps to get rid of these germs, meaning that we won't smell unpleasant even when we are sweaty.

IT IS IMPORTANT THAT THE TOWEL THAT WE USE TO DRY OURSELVES IS CLEAN AND DRY.

WHAT IS THE BEST WAY TO KEEP CLEAN?

The best way to keep clean is by washing in a bath or shower with soap and water. It is a good idea to use a sponge or a flannel to wash because these things help to remove more dirt and dead skin.

BRUSHING YOUR TEETH

TO KEEP YOUR TEETH CLEAN, YOU SHOULD BRUSH THEM TWICE EVERY DAY.

HEALTHY

WHAT ARE RELATIONSHIPS?

Human beings are social animals, which means that we are supposed to live in groups and spend time with other people. Our relationships are the connections that we have to people that we spend time with. We have many different relationships throughout our lives and each one is different.

WHO DO WE HAVE RELATIONSHIPS WITH?

Possibly the most important relationships that we have are with our families and friends, but we also have important relationships with other people such as teachers, leaders of after-school clubs and our friends' parents. We might also have relationships with adults such as doctors or health professionals. Some children also have relationships with childminders or neighbours who help to look after them.

Relationships

FAMILIES

Families come in all different shapes and sizes. Many children and young adults live with their parents and **SIBLINGS**. Some children's parents are no longer together, so they may live with only one parent. Some people also have step-parents and step-siblings. Some children don't live with their parents at all. Instead, they might live with their grandparents or another guardian. Whoever we live with, it is important to have healthy relationships with them.

WHAT IS A HEALTHY RELATIONSHIP?

Each of our relationships is different and special. They can change over time and often have their ups and downs. It is perfectly normal for people to argue at times, especially when they spend a lot of time together. However, it is not normal to feel frightened or scared in a relationship.

PARENTS

Your home should be a place where you feel safe. The adults in your home love you and you love them back. However, as you get older you may find that you don't always agree with your parents. They may get cross with you sometimes for the things that you do. They might tell you off or punish you by stopping you from doing something that you enjoy. You may feel angry towards them sometimes because you do not like their rules or the decisions that they make. This is a normal part of growing up.

PARENTS ARE USUALLY GOOD PEOPLE TO DISCUSS YOUR PROBLEMS WITH AS THEY ARE OFTEN ABLE TO SUGGEST WAYS OF SOLVING THEM.

HAPPY HOME

It is important that we try to remember just how much our parents do for us. Most parents are very loving and kind and always try to do the best for their children. Looking after children is hard work at times and it can cost a lot of money. Because of this, it might make your parents happy if you let them know how much you enjoy all the things that they do for you. Doing jobs around your house is a great way to help your **CAREGIVER**.

If you are unhappy with something that your parent has said or done, try to talk about it with them in a grown-up way without getting angry or shouting.

SIBLINGS

Many children live with their siblings. You might have older siblings, younger siblings or both. Some children don't have any siblings at all while others have many. Your relationship with your siblings was probably one of the first relationships that you ever made. Many siblings play together at home and get on well. Relationships with siblings are some of the best and most important relationships that a person can have.

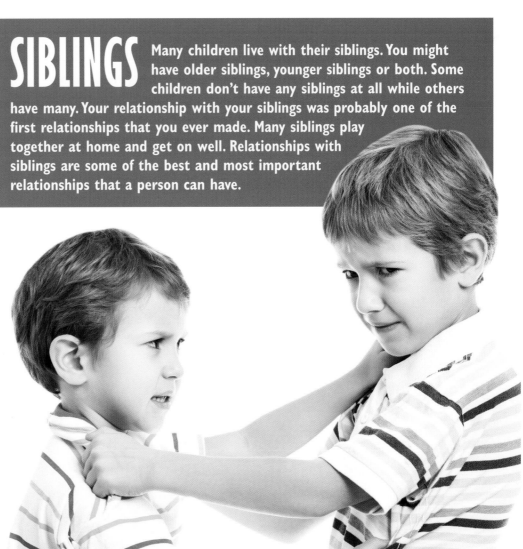

SOMETIMES IT CAN BE HARD TO LIVE WITH YOUR SIBLINGS BUT MOST SIBLINGS GET ON VERY WELL WHEN THEY ARE ADULTS.

It is quite normal for siblings to struggle to get on at times. Your brother or sister might be very different to you and they might have a different relationship with your parents. It is normal to be angry with your siblings sometimes. Try to talk through what is upsetting you with your sibling and try to also think about what they might be feeling. Sometimes your parents might be able to help you with any problems that you are having with your siblings.

FAMILIES

Sometimes families change and people have to live with a new step-father or step-mother. It can sometimes be difficult to deal with new step-parents or siblings. It can be helpful to try to see new people in your life as a **POSITIVE** thing. It is important to have good relationships with everyone, including step-parents, and it can be fun to have new relatives.

EXTENDED FAMILY

Many children also have good relationships with their grandparents, aunts and uncles. These adults often care for you deeply and they might have more time to do things with you. They can be helpful people to talk to if you have a problem that you feel that you can't talk to your parents about.

COUSINS ARE OFTEN A SIMILAR AGE TO YOU AND CAN BE GREAT FRIENDS.

FRIENDS

Relationships with friends are very important. Many people spend a lot of time with their friends while at school. You might even see some of your friends outside of school, either at clubs or by going to their houses. Having lots of friends can be very fun and you will have a different relationship with each friend that you make.

RELATIONSHIPS OFTEN CHANGE AS WE GROW OLDER

SOMETIMES GOOD FRIENDS STOP SEEING EACH OTHER AND START TO SPEND TIME WITH OTHER FRIENDS INSTEAD. THIS IS A NORMAL PART OF GROWING UP.

GOOD FRIENDS

Good friends can be friends for life. A good friend will accept you for who you are and they will respect you for the choices that you make. As with all relationships, friends can sometimes argue or fall out, but good friends should always try to fix their problems.

ISSUES WITH

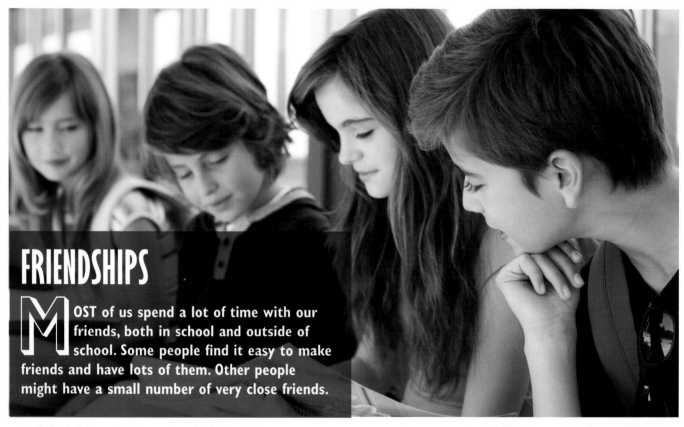

FRIENDSHIPS

MOST of us spend a lot of time with our friends, both in school and outside of school. Some people find it easy to make friends and have lots of them. Other people might have a small number of very close friends.

JEALOUSY

We all feel jealous sometimes, which is the feeling you get when someone has something that you want. People might be jealous of you because you own something that they wish that they had or because they think that you are better than them at something. Jealousy can cause problems between friends and can sometimes make people very angry.

Friends FALLING OUT

When we are good friends with somebody, it is not unusual for us to fall out with them. This often happens because we spend a lot of time with the person and we trust them enough to tell them how we feel. Sometimes these disagreements can lead to friends falling out with each other. This might result in them not spending time together or even not speaking to each other for a time.

IF YOUR FRIEND GETS ANGRY WITH YOU AND TRIES TO MAKE OTHER PEOPLE NOT LIKE YOU, THEN THEY MIGHT NOT BE A TRUE FRIEND AT ALL.

RESOLVING FALL OUTS

Friends usually fall out because one or both of them is feeling angry about something. Someone who is feeling angry usually needs to be given some time to calm down. If you know that you have done something wrong, it is important to apologise, but once you have done this you may still need to wait a little time before you are forgiven. If a friend apologises to you, try to accept their apology. Most arguments are not worth losing a friend over.

PRESSURE

Sometimes we feel like we have to do something because our friends are doing it. It might be something that we are not comfortable with or that we know is wrong. It can be hard to say no to our friends at times, especially if there is more than one of them. In these situations, remember that you are your own person and that you make the decisions about what actions you do. If you don't want to do something, you don't have to and true friends will accept your decision.

DIFFERENCES

We are all different and unique. While we often have many things in common with our friends, we are also quite different from them. Try to see the differences between you and your friends as good a thing. Life would be boring if we all thought and acted in the exact same way! It is good for us to be friends with lots of different people as it can help us to experience more of what life has to offer.

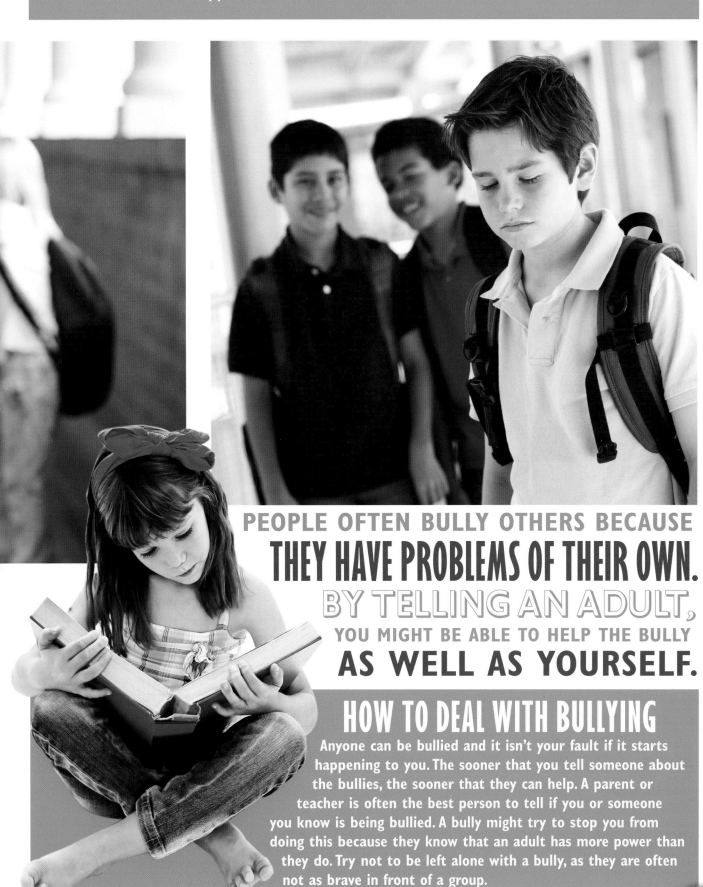

BULLYING

Bullying is when a person or group **PERSISTENTLY** hurts someone else on purpose. The hurt can be physical, but it might also be non-physical. Physical bullying is when someone hurts your body, whereas non-physical bullying is usually **VERBAL** and can include name-calling and spreading lies. Bullying doesn't only happen at school, it can also happen on the internet and over texts.

PEOPLE OFTEN BULLY OTHERS BECAUSE
THEY HAVE PROBLEMS OF THEIR OWN.
BY TELLING AN ADULT,
YOU MIGHT BE ABLE TO HELP THE BULLY
AS WELL AS YOURSELF.

HOW TO DEAL WITH BULLYING

Anyone can be bullied and it isn't your fault if it starts happening to you. The sooner that you tell someone about the bullies, the sooner that they can help. A parent or teacher is often the best person to tell if you or someone you know is being bullied. A bully might try to stop you from doing this because they know that an adult has more power than they do. Try not to be left alone with a bully, as they are often not as brave in front of a group.

RESPECTING

WHAT IS RESPECTING YOURSELF?

IF we have respect for someone, it means that we admire the things that they do. It also means that we consider their thoughts and feelings when choosing our own words and actions. In order to respect ourselves, we must admire ourselves and consider our own feelings, thoughts and desires.

BODY IMAGE

It is perfectly normal to think about the way that we look. It can be very easy to compare the way that you look to the way that others look and to feel that you are somehow not as good as them. Remember, how we look on the outside is not as important as who we are on the inside.

Yourself

RELATIONSHIPS

The relationships that you have while you are growing up aren't always easy. There may be times when your friends or siblings cause you to **DOUBT** yourself and it is during these times that it is important to respect yourself. Remember to be kind to yourself and to not take too much notice of what others say.

IT IS A GOOD IDEA TO DISCUSS YOUR RELATIONSHIPS WITH AN ADULT, SUCH AS A PARENT OR TEACHER.

DIFFERENT RELATIONSHIPS

Nearing the end of school, some children start to take an interest in relationships. They might even decide that they want a boyfriend or a girlfriend. If you do have a boyfriend or a girlfriend, it is important that you respect them and yourself. You can respect yourself by looking after your body and making the right choices.

HEALTHY
BALANCE

THE way that we eat can have a huge impact on our bodies; the more healthy food that we put into our bodies, the healthier they will become. Part of respecting ourselves is thinking about what we eat and making informed choices about it.

CARBOHYDRATES

PROTEIN

SUG

THE BALANCED PLATE

There are five main food groups and it is important that we eat food from all of them in order to have a balanced and healthy diet. The Balanced Plate is a diagram that shows us how much of each food group we should eat at every meal.

Eating

BODY WEIGHT

We all have different body shapes and what is a healthy body weight for one person may not be healthy for someone else. Eating healthily and exercising can help you maintain a body weight that is healthy for you.

FRUITS AND VEGETABLES

DAIRY

VARIETY

It is good for us to have a varied diet and to try to not eat the same foods too often. As we get older, our tastes change, so it is important that we try foods again even if we didn't like their taste in the past.

EXERCISE

CHILDREN SHOULD TRY TO EXERCISE FOR ONE HOUR A DAY.

WHICH EXERCISE?

Any activity that makes your heart beat quickly is a form of exercise. You might already be doing lots of exercise without even realising it! Walking to school or to a friend's house are both types of exercise. Running around on the playground or at the park will also get your heart pumping more quickly. It is good to vary the types of exercise that you do, so if you do a lot of walking, why not go on a bike ride with a friend or go swimming with your family?

WHY SHOULD WE DO IT?

NOT only is exercise very good for our bodies but it also helps us to feel good about ourselves. Exercising causes the brain to release endorphins, which are hormones that make us feel happy. Most forms of exercise are social, like sport, meaning that we can spend time with our friends while doing exercise.

Glossary

anxious	worried
caffeine	a substance found in tea, coffee and soft drinks that keeps us awake
caregiver	an adult who helps to look after someone
cease	not continue
glands	organs in the body that release substances that the body needs
hormones	substances made in the body that control growth and emotions
informed choices	knowing all the options before you make a choice
organised	good at preparing things in advance
organisms	life forms, including animals, plants and germs
persistently	keeps trying
physical	to do with the body
positive	good and desirable
siblings	brothers and sisters
unique	unlike anything else
verbal	in the form of words

Index

PHOTO CREDITS

Photocredits: Abbreviations: l–left, r–right, b–bottom, t–top, c–centre, m–middle.
Front Cover – mama_mia. 2 – Gladskikh Tatiana. 4–5tm – jordache. 4br – Duplass. 4ml – www.BillionPhotos.com. 5br – pathdoc. 5tr – amenic181. 6ml – Oksana Kuzmina. 6tl – Martin Novak. 6–7bm – karelnoppe. 7m – Pressmaster. 8t – Olga Bogatyrenko. 8br – kate_ku. 9t – Olga Sapegina. 9mr – IAKOBCHUK VIACHESLAV. 10bl – Kalmatsuy. 10–11m – Didecs. 11br – Elena Stepanova. 12 – Oleg Golovnev. 13m – Pressmaster. 13br – Ermolaev Alexander. 14–15m – VaLiza. 14bl – Suzanne Tucker. 15m – Jorg Hackemann. 15tr – Alexander Trinitatov. 15br – Ilya Andriyanov. 16–17m – Monkey Business Images. 16br – Kalmatsuy. 17mr – Monkey Business Images. 17br – Mila May. 18t –Yuganov Konstantin. 19m – Ilya Andriyanov. 19bl – wavebreakmedia. 20t – Kinga. 20br – Rob Hainer. 21tr – BlueOrange Studio. 21b – Zurijeta. 22t – Joana Lopes. 22b – Oleg Mikhaylov. 23t – SpeedKingz. 23br – wavebreakmedia. 24m – wavebreakmedia. 24br – Monkey Business Images. 25m – Monkey Business Images. 25bl – Jeka. 26–27m – lightwavemedia. 26bl – Vadim Ponomarenko. 27br – Jiri Hera. 28–29m – ifong. 28ml – Boris Bulychev. 29mr – Zurijeta. 30ml – Robert Kneschke. 30br –Poznyakov.
Images are courtesy of Shutterstock.com. With thanks to Getty Images, Thinkstock Photo and iStockphoto.